1 MONTH FREE READING

at

www.ForgottenBooks.com

By purchasing this book you are eligible for one month membership to ForgottenBooks.com, giving you unlimited access to our entire collection of over 700,000 titles via our web site and mobile apps.

To claim your free month visit: www.forgottenbooks.com/free299138

* Offer is valid for 45 days from date of purchase. Terms and conditions apply.

English
Français
Deutsche
Italiano
Español
Português

www.forgottenbooks.com

Mythology Photography **Fiction**
Fishing Christianity **Art** Cooking
Essays Buddhism Freemasonry
Medicine **Biology** Music **Ancient Egypt** Evolution Carpentry Physics
Dance Geology **Mathematics** Fitness
Shakespeare **Folklore** Yoga Marketing
Confidence Immortality Biographies
Poetry **Psychology** Witchcraft
Electronics Chemistry History **Law**
Accounting **Philosophy** Anthropology
Alchemy Drama Quantum Mechanics
Atheism Sexual Health **Ancient History**
Entrepreneurship Languages Sport
Paleontology Needlework Islam
Metaphysics Investment Archaeology
Parenting Statistics Criminology
Motivational

797,885 Books
are available to read at

Forgotten Books

www.ForgottenBooks.com

Forgotten Books' App
Available for mobile, tablet & eReader

ISBN 978-1-332-21358-0
PIBN 10299138

This book is a reproduction of an important historical work. Forgotten Books uses state-of-the-art technology to digitally reconstruct the work, preserving the original format whilst repairing imperfections present in the aged copy. In rare cases, an imperfection in the original, such as a blemish or missing page, may be replicated in our edition. We do, however, repair the vast majority of imperfections successfully; any imperfections that remain are intentionally left to preserve the state of such historical works.

Forgotten Books is a registered trademark of FB &c Ltd.
Copyright © 2015 FB &c Ltd.
FB &c Ltd, Dalton House, 60 Windsor Avenue, London, SW19 2RR.
Company number 08720141. Registered in England and Wales.

For support please visit www.forgottenbooks.com

Binding is in Blue Cloth with Cover Design Stamped in Gold

PRICE $2.00 NET

Size, 5⅜ x 8 inches;
600 Pages
115 Full Page Plates
Including a Series of
Cartoons by
Homer C. Davenport

America's National Game
By A. G. SPALDING
PRICE, $2.00 NET

A book of 600 pages, profusely illustrated with over 100 full page engravings, and having sixteen forceful cartoons by Homer C. Davenport, the famous American artist.

No man in America is better equipped to write on all the varied phases of the National Game than is A. G. Spalding. His observation and experience began when the game was young. He gained fame as a pitcher forty years ago, winning a record as player that has never yet been equalled. He was associated with the management of the pastime through trying years of struggle against prevailing evils. He opposed the gamblers; he fought to eradicate drunkenness; he urged and introduced new and higher ideals for the sport; he was quick to see that ball playing and the business management of clubs, at the same time and by the same men, were impracticable; he knew that ball players might be quite competent as magnates, but not while playing the game; he was in the forefront of the fight against syndicating Base Ball and making of a Nation's pastime a sordid Trust; he was the pioneer to lead competing American Base Ball teams to a foreign land; he took two champion teams to Great Britain in 1874, and two others on a tour of the world in 1888-9; he was present at the birth of the National League, and has done as much as any living American to uphold and prolong the life of this great pioneer Base Ball organization.

When A. G. Spalding talks about America's National Game he speaks by authority of that he does know, because he has been in the councils of the management whenever there have been times of strenuous endeavor to purge it from abuses and keep it clean for the people of America —young and old.

In this work Mr. Spalding, after explaining the causes that led him into the undertaking, begins with the inception of the sport; shows how it developed, by natural stages from a boy with a ball to eighteen men, ball, bats and bases; gives credit for the first scientific application of system to the playing of the game to Abner Doubleday, of Cooperstown, N. Y.: treats of the first Base Ball club; shows how rowdyism terrorized the sport in its early days; how gambling and drunkenness brought the pastime into disfavor with the masses, and how early organizations were unable to control the evils that insidiously crept in. He then draws a series of very forceful pictures of the struggle to eradicate gambling, drunkenness and kindred evils, and shows how the efforts of strong men accomplished the salvation of the great American game and placed it in the position it occupies to-day—the most popular outdoor pastime in the world.

Interspersed throughout this interesting book are reminiscences of Mr. Spalding's own personal observations and experiences in the game as player, manager and magnate, covering a period of many years. Some of these stories deal with events of great import to Base Ball, and others have to do with personal acts and characteristics of players prominent in the game in earlier days—old time favorites like Harry and George Wright, A. C. Anson, Mike Kelly, Billy Sunday and others.

This book should be in the library of every father in the land, for it shows how his boy may be built up physically and morally through a high-class pastime. It should be in the hands of every lad in America, for it demonstrates the possibilities to American youth of rising to heights of eminent material success through a determined adherence to things that make for the upbuilding of character in organizations as well as of men.

Mailed postpaid on receipt of price by any Spalding store (see list on inside front cover), or by the publishers,

AMERICAN SPORTS PUBLISHING COMPANY
21 Warren Street, New York

SPALDING ATHLETIC LIBRARY

Giving the Titles of all Spalding Athletic Library Books now in print, grouped for ready reference

SPALDING OFFICIAL ANNUALS

No.	
1	Spalding's Official Base Ball Guide
1A	Spalding's Official Base Ball Record
1C	Spalding's Official College Base Ball Annual
2	Spalding's Official Foot Ball Guide
2A	Spalding's Official Soccer Foot Ball Guide
4	Spalding's Official Lawn Tennis Annual
6	Spalding's Official Ice Hockey Guide
7	Spalding's Official Basket Ball Guide
7A	Spalding's Official Women's Basket Ball Guide
8	Spalding's Official Lacrosse Guide
9	Spalding's Official Indoor Base Ball Guide
12A	Spalding's Official Athletic Rules

Group I. Base Ball
No. 1 Spalding's Official Base Ball Guide.
No. 1A Official Base Ball Record.
No. 1C College Base Ball Annual.
No. 202 How to Play Base Ball.
No. 223 How to Bat.
No. 232 How to Run Bases.
No. 230 How to Pitch.
No. 229 How to Catch.
No. 225 How to Play First Base.
No. 226 How to Play Second Base.
No. 227 How to Play Third Base.
No. 228 How to Play Shortstop.
No. 224 How to Play the Outfield.
No. 231 { How to Organize a Base Ball League. [Club. How to Organize a Base Ball How to Manage a Base Ball Club. How to Train a Base Ball Team How to Captain a Base Ball How to Umpire a Game. [Team Technical Base Ball Terms.
No. 219 Ready Reckoner of Base Ball Percentages.
No. 350 How to Score.

BASE BALL AUXILIARIES
No. 355 Minor League Base Ball Guide
No. 356 Official Book National League of Prof. Base Ball Clubs.
No. 340 Official Handbook National Playground Ball Ass'n.

Group II. Foot Ball
No. 2 Spalding's Official Foot Ball Guide
No. 344 A Digest of the Foot Ball Rules
No. 324 How to Play Foot Ball.
No. 2A Spalding's Official Soccer Foot Ball Guide.
No. 286 How to Play Soccer.
No. 335 How to Play Rugby.

FOOT BALL AUXILIARY
No. 351 Official Rugby Foot Ball Guide

Group IV. Lawn Tennis
No. 4 Spalding's Official Lawn Tennis Annual.
No. 157 How to Play Lawn Tennis.
No. 354 Official Handbook National Squash Tennis Association.

Group VI. Hockey
No. 6 Spalding's Official Ice Hockey Guide.
No. 154 Field Hockey.
No. 180 Ring Hockey.

Group VII. Basket Ball
No. 7 Spalding's Official Basket Ball Guide.
No. 7A Spalding's Official Women's Basket Ball Guide.
No. 193 How to Play Basket Ball.

BASKET BALL AUXILIARY
No. 353 Official Collegiate Basket Ball Handbook.

Group VIII. Lacrosse
No. 8 Spalding's Official Lacrosse Guide
No. 201 How to Play Lacrosse.

Group IX. Indoor Base Ball
No. 9 Spalding's Official Indoor Base Ball Guide.

Group X. Polo
No. 129 Water Polo.
No. 199 Equestrian Polo.

Group XI. Miscellaneous Games
No. 248 Archery.   No. 138 Croquet.
No. 271 Roque.
No. 194 { Racquets. Squash-Racquets. Court Tennis.
No. 13 Hand Ball.   No. 167 Quoits.
No. 170 Push Ball.   No. 14 Curling.
No. 207 Lawn Bowls.
No. 188 { Lawn Hockey. Parlor Hockey. Garden Hockey. Lawn Games.
No. 189 Children's Games.
No. 341 How to Bowl.

ANY OF THE ABOVE BOOKS MAILED POSTPAID UPON RECEIPT OF 10 CENTS

Group XII. Athletics
- No. 12A Spalding's Official Athletic Rules.
- No. 27 College Athletics.
- No. 182 All Around Athletics.
- No. 156 Athletes' Guide.
- No. 87 Athletic Primer.
- No. 273 Olympic Games at Athens, 1906
- No. 252 How to Sprint.
- No. 255 How to Run 100 Yards.
- No. 174 Distance and Cross Country Running. [Thrower.
- No. 259 How to Become a Weight
- No. 55 Official Sporting Rules.
- No. 246 Athletic Training for School-
- No. 317 Marathon Running. [boys.
- No. 331 Schoolyard Athletics.
- No. 342 Walking for Health and Competition.

ATHLETIC AUXILIARIES
- No. 357 Intercollegiate Official Hand-
- No. 314 Girls' Athletics. [book.
- No. 302 Y. M. C. A. Official Handbook.
- No. 313 Public Schools Athletic League Official Handbook.
- No. 308 Official Handbook New York Interscholastic A. A.

Group XIII. Athletic Accomplishments
- No. 177 How to Swim.
- No. 296 Speed Swimming.
- No. 128 How to Row.
- No. 209 How to Become a Skater.
- No. 178 How to Train for Bicycling.
- No. 23 Canoeing.
- No. 282 Roller Skating Guide.

Group XIV. Manly Sports
- No. 18 Fencing. (By Breck.)
- No. 162 Boxing.
- No. 165 Fencing. (By Senac.)

Group XIV. Manly Sports—Co
- No. 236 How to Wrestle.
- No. 102 Ground Tumbling
- No. 200 Dumb Bell Exercises.
- No. 143 Indian Clubs and Dumb Bell
- No. 262 Medicine Ball Exercises.
- No. 29 Pulley Weight Exercises.
- No. 191 How to Punch the Bag.
- No. 289 Tumbling for Amateurs.

Group XV. Gymnastic
- No. 104 Grading of Gymnastic Exercises. [Dumb Bell Drill
- No. 214 Graded Calisthenics an
- No. 254 Barnjum Bar Bell Drill. [Gam
- No. 158 Indoor and Outdoor Gymnast
- No. 124 How to Become a Gymnast.
- No. 287 Fancy Dumb Bell and Marcing Drills. [Apparatu
- No. 327 Pyramid Building Witho
- No. 328 Exercises on the Parallel Bar
- No. 329 Pyramid Building wi Wands, Chairs and Ladder
- No. 345 Official Handbook I. C. A. Gymnasts of America.

Group XVI. Physical Cultur
- No. 161 10 Minutes' Exercise for Bus Men. [and Care of the Bod
- No. 149 Scientific Physical Trainin
- No. 208 Physical Education and H
- No. 185 Hints on Health. [gien
- No. 213 285 Health Answers.
- No. 238 Muscle Building.
- No. 234 School Tactics and Maze Ru
- No. 261 Tensing Exercises. [nin
- No. 285 Health by Muscular Gymnastics. [nastic
- No. 288 Indigestion Treated by Gym
- No. 325 Twenty-Minute Exercises.
- No. 330 Physical Training for th School and Class Room.

ANY OF THE ABOVE BOOKS MAILED POSTPAID UPON RECEIPT OF 10 CENTS

Spalding "Red Cover" Series of Athletic Handbook

No. 1R.	Spalding's Official Athletic Almanac.	Price 25c
No. 2R.	Strokes and Science of Lawn Tennis.	Price 25c
No. 3R.	Spalding's Official Golf Guide.	Price 25c
No. 4R.	How to Play Golf.	Price 25c
No. 5R.	Spalding's Official Cricket Guide.	Price 25c
No. 6R.	Cricket and How to Play It.	Price 25c
No. 7R.	Physical Training Simplified.	Price 25c
No. 8R.	The Art of Skating.	Price 25c
No. 9R.	How to Live 100 Years.	Price 25c
No. 10R.	Single Stick Drill.	Price 25c
No. 11R.	Fencing Foil Work Illustrated.	Price 25c
No. 12R.	Exercises on the Side Horse.	Price 25c
No. 13R.	Horizontal Bar Exercises.	Price 25c
No. 14R.	Trapeze, Long Horse and Rope Exercises.	Price 25c
No. 15R.	Exercises on the Flying Rings.	Price 25c
No. 16R.	Team Wand Drill.	Price 25c
No. 17R.	Olympic Games, Stockholm, 1912.	Price 25c
No. 18R.	Wrestling.	Price 25c
No. 19R.	Professional Wrestling.	Price 25c
No. 20R.	How to Play Ice Hockey.	Price 25c
No. 21R.	Jiu Jitsu.	Price 25c
No. 22R.	How to Swing Indian Clubs.	Price 25c
No. 23R.	Get Well; Keep Well.	Price 25c

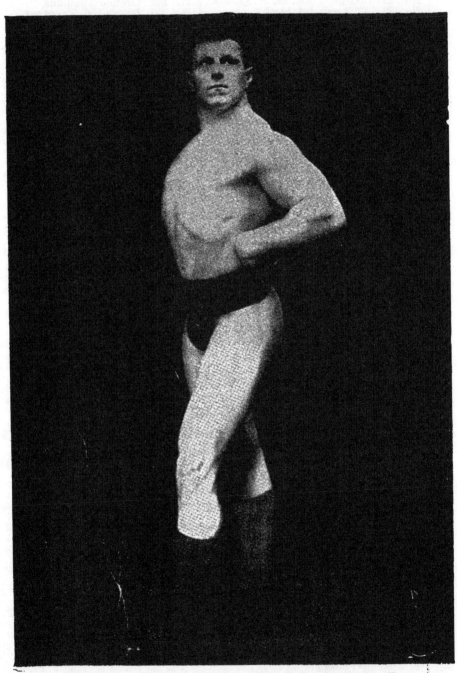

Georges Hackenschmidt, "The Russian Lion."

Spalding "Red Cover" Series of
Athletic Handbooks
No. 18R

WRESTLING

CATCH-AS-CATCH-CAN STYLE

BY

E. Hitchcock, Jr., M. D.
Cornell University, Ithaca, N. Y.

AND

R. F. Nelligan
Amherst College, Amherst, Mass.

PUBLISHED BY
AMERICAN SPORTS PUBLISHING
COMPANY
21 WARREN STREET, NEW YORK

COPYRIGHT, 1912
BY
AMERICAN SPORTS PUBLISHING COMPANY
NEW YORK

WRESTLING

CATCH-AS-CATCH-CAN

THIS style is selected for illustration because it is the most universal, and practically comprises all the other forms. It is the most natural method, the most effective under all circumstances, and requires no special preparation in the way of clothing.

The attempt has not been made here to touch upon all the locks and combinations, since there is practically no limit to them, but rather to show the most common and useful, and by presenting them graphically, to show the diverse possibilities of this form of wrestling.

As a physical exercise there is no sport which calls for so much strength, endurance and agility, combined with cool judgment; and with men who love to oppose their strength to that of others, no sport is so popular.

Wrestling does offer opportunities for ungentlemanly and unsportsmanlike work, but so do all other competitive athletics. It is to the lover of sport, the true amateur, our little work is offered.

In the following illustrations, certain holds, breaks and doubles are described, which the amateur will not use because they are brutal; but while he discards them in all friendly competition, still he should know their danger and value, and be able to apply them if forced into unwelcome encounter with a man who is not inspired by the finer feelings of the amateur. Personal encounters forced upon one in defense of life or property are by no means always settled by fist or weapon, and a knowledge of the Strangle, Nelson or Backhammer has often enabled a man to successfully defend himself.

Since it is not claimed that this is a "Complete Guide to Wrestling," we have no apologies to offer. It is intended as an aid to beginners, and it is also hoped that those well trained in the sport may find in our illustrations some ideas which may prove of practical use to them.

INSTRUCTIONS

❧ ❧ ❧

1. The Referee's Hold

Sometimes given by the Referee when the men fail to take a Hold. The other Hold given under these circumstances is what is known as "One over and one under." Here each has his left arm over his opponent's shoulder, and the right under his arm.

NOTE.—The following directions for making the Holds are addressed to the aggressor; those for the Stops, Breaks and Doubles to his opponent.

2. Both Legs Hold and Stop

If your opponent's legs are close together (which will happen only in the case of a novice), step forward and grasp around his knees, stand erect, throw him backward over your shoulder, turn, fall with him and force the two points down. To Stop this Throw, bend forward after the Leg Hold has been taken, and before he lifts clasp him around the waist and lift his legs from the floor.

NOTE.—Here, as in all other Breaks, Doubles and Stops, following your successful escape, you will take such a Hold as the position of your opponent makes possible.

3. Break for Both Legs Hold

Place your hands on the back of his head, throw your weight on it, force him to the floor and fall

with him, looking for a chance for a Hold after he is on the floor.

4. Leg and Inside Back Heel, with Stop

Catch his nearest leg with both hands, step inside

and Back Heel his other leg. If he hugs you close,

lift and throw him over your head. To Stop it, throw your arm about his neck and squeeze hard, grasping your wrist with your free hand.

NOTE.—This Stop, as is the case with many other Stops and Holds following, is for punishment only. Punishment Holds rarely result in actual falls, but they do not infrequently result in your opponent giving you the Fall by admitting his unwillingness to remain in the position in which you have placed him.

5. Shoulder Twist

Place one hand beneath his elbow, and with the

other grasp his wrist. Twist his shoulder and push backward.

6. Arm Up the Back, with Brake On

The opening for this Hold is offered in such a position as that shown in No. 5. Using wrist and elbow for leverage, force his arm up his back, let go the elbow and put the Brake on—which means

to slip your forearm under and inside his nearest arm, thus giving you absolute and easy control of it. Let go the wrist, bear down on his neck and force his arm up until he acknowledges the Fall. For punishment.

7. Back Strangle

Step behind and put on a Full Strangle Lock, and pull him backward.

NOTE.—A Strangle Lock always means the placing of one forearm across the front of your opponent's neck. This may or may not be strengthened by the use of the other arm. In the Full Strangle, one arm is in front and the other behind his neck,

while in the Half Strangle only one arm is used on the neck. The object of the Strangle is indicated by its name.

8. Possible Double for Back Strangle
Before he has time to pull you back, get your

nip in and stop the Strangle, catch him by the

elbows, bend forward and throw him over your back.

9. Waist Lock, and Double by Strangle and Leg Grapevine

Clasp around his waist, lift and throw. To Double, get Full Strangle and at the same time a Leg Grapevine. Force him backward and fall with him.

NOTE —The Grapevine is the twining of an arm or leg about his arm or leg.

10. Strangle and Outside Back Heel

Get a Strangle, step in and place your heel outside and back of his nearest foot. Push him backward and fall with him.

11. Double for Strangle and Outside Back Heel

Step back before he gets the Back Heel, and at

the same time put on a Waist Lock. Lift and throw him.

12. Strangle and Inside Leg Lock

Get a Strangle, and at the same time step in and get the Inside Leg Lock. Lift with your leg and

arms, force backward and fall with him. To Stop it, before he Locks your leg, **step back, lift and throw him, as in No. 11.**

13. Stop for Waist Lock

Place your hand on his forehead and snap his

head back. This could be followed by a Buttock Throw, as in No. 53.

14. Waist Lock

Grasp your opponent around the body, try to lift

and throw. When caught in this position, to

Double, throw your arms outside of your opponent's, clasp your hands, go to your knees, thus bringing him to his knees, and try to roll him over.

15. Strangle from Behind, on the Floor

For Punishment.

16. Strangle from the Front, on the Floor

For Punishment.

17. Strangle, or Hang, with Half Nelson from the Front, on the Floor

Force his head down with your left hand (or with your right, if from the other side), thrust your

right arm under his left and place your right hand on his head. Crowd your left forearm against his neck in front. Punishment.

18. Foot and Neck, on the Floor

Catch his nearest foot, reach under his neck, catch opposite shoulder and roll him over.

NOTE.---The Fall may sometimes be made, but usually the hold is for punishment.

19. Half Strangle and Crotch

Get a Half Strangle, catch one thigh from inside force him backward and fall with him.

20. Stop for Half Strangle and Crotch, Standing

When he attempts to place his forearm across your neck, grasp his wrist and elbow and put on a Shoulder Twist, as in No. 5.

21. Waist Lock from Behind and Double by Head over Shoulder

Get a Waist Lock from behind and throw. To

Double, **reach up** and catch around his neck, draw his head forward, go down on your knees, roll over forward as in No. 22, pulling him with you. Fall on top of him.

NOTE.—An expert would not allow his head to be near enough for this Double.

22. A Portion of Head over Shoulder—No. 21.

23. Bridge to Stop the Fall from Head Over Shoulder—A continuation of No. 22.

24. Half Nelson from the Front and Leg Lock, on the Floor

Get a Half Nelson, and while turning him over turn your back towards him and pass your arm

outside and under his opposite leg. Bring his head and knee as near together as possible, and roll him over.

25. Stop for Half Nelson from Behind, on the Floor.

When he attempts to get his arm under yours, pin it to your side with your elbow and throw your head back.

NOTE.—The Half Nelson from in front necessitates your thrusting your right arm under his left, or your left under his right, while from behind, your right is under his right, etc.

26. Locked Half Nelson, from Behind

Get a Half Nelson, reach under with your free hand, lock the fingers of both hands or clasp your

own wrist, place your head under his arm, pull his head under, roll him over and fall on him.

27. Spin Out of a Half Nelson

Throw your feet in the air and spin around to the other side, using your head for a pivot.

28. Stop for a Spin

Catch him around the waist with your free arm and so stop his turning.

29. Half Nelson and Hold Outside of Leg, Standing

Get a Half Nelson, reach over and place your free hand between his legs from behind, lift up, roll over and fall with him.

30. Half Nelson and Leg, Standing

Get Half Nelson from behind, pull his head down, catch his opposite leg, double him up and clasp hands, lift up, throw him forward and fall with him.

31. Double for Half Nelson from Behind, on the Floor

If his head is near enough, reach your arm about his neck, pull him over your back and roll over with him.

32. Half Nelson on Neck and Leg

Grasp his foot when he is face down, drop your knee on his leg just above his knee to hold the leg firm, then bend his knee and get a Half Nelson on

his foot. Watch your chance and slip your free arm under his nearest arm, and put a Half Nelson on his neck. Roll him over, or take your time for punishment.

33. Half Nelson and Crotch, on the Floor

Get a Half Nelson from behind, catch his leg high up, and roll him over head first.

34. Half Nelson from Behind and Outside Leg, on the Floor

Get a Half Nelson, reach under and between his legs, grasp opposite thigh, roll him over and fall with him.

35. Back Hammer and Half Nelson from Behind, on the Floor

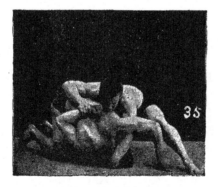

If possible, get the Half Nelson first, then reach over and catch the farthest wrist and force it up his back. Roll him over or punish.

36. Full Nelson, Standing

If you find yourself behind him, reach under both arms and clasp your arms as high up around his neck as possible, thus putting on the Full Nelson.

To Double this hold, while he is getting the Nelson or even sometimes after he has got it, pinion his arms to your sides with your elbows, go down on your knees and roll him over to the side, as in Nos. 37 and 42.

37. Double for Full Nelson, Standing

38. Neck Bend and Back Heel

Usually got from a Waist Hold. Reach up and clasp your hands across his face, force his head back and Back Heel him.

39. Full Nelson from the Front, on the Floor

Get a Half Nelson first and follow with the other arm.

40. A Possible Double for a Full Nelson from the Front, on the Floor

Draw your knees well up, secure his arms to your sides with your elbows, sit up and fall over backwards, throwing him over your shoulders.

41. Full Nelson from Behind, on the Floor

Get a Half Nelson, force his head down and get a Half Nelson with the other arm.

NOTE.—This Hold, with the Strangles, is barred in amateur contests.

42. Double for Full Nelson

Pin his arms to your sides and roll over sideways.

43. Arm Up the Back with Brake On, on the Floor

See No. 6.

44. Arm Up the Back, Brake On, and Strangle, on the Floor

Force his arm up his back and put the Brake on. Get a Strangle with your other arm, clasp your hands together and squeeze. Punishment.

45. Flying Mare

Grasp his wrist with both hands, twitch him towards you, turn and lift his arm with palm down

on your shoulder. Use the arm for a lever and throw him over your shoulder.

46. Flying Mare

Grasp his other arm (see 45), keep his palm up, and throw him as before.

47. Arm Grapevine and Cross Buttock

Grasp his wrist with both hands, twitch him towards you, turn, step outside and behind his

nearest leg, twine your arm about his and throw him forward over your hip.

48. Break for a Bridge

Place your forearm across his neck and press your other elbow against the pit of his stomach.

NOTE.—Many Falls can be stopped by a Bridge, which is holding the shoulders up from the floor by supporting the body on the head and feet. The Bridge can be strengthened by hands on the hips and elbows on the floor.

49. Buttock or Hip Lock

Grasp him about the neck, at the same time pulling him forward and throwing him over your hip. Fall with him.

50. Double for Buttock or Hip Lock

Before he has time to lift you over his hip, drop your shoulder in front of his body, grasp his legs, lift up and fall with him, as in No. 51.

51. Finish of Double for Buttock No. 50.

52. Another Double for Buttock

Catch him around the neck and by his nearest leg, or place your nearest arm across the front of his neck, grasp his leg, lift up and throw backward.

53. Buttock and Outside Leg Lock.

Catch him around the neck, pull him forward, step outside his leg and force him over. This can

be Stopped and Doubled, before he has stepped in, by catching him around the waist, lifting and throwing him as in No. 54.

54. Double for Buttock.

Catch him around the waist, lift and throw

55. Cross Buttock.

Catch him around the neck, or under his arm and over his neck, step well behind and throw him over your hip.

56. Cornwall Heave.

Turn sideways, and with your nearest arm grasp him around the body in front while the other arm grasps around him behind. Lift and throw back-

wards and fall with him. An attempt to stop it would be with a Neck Hold, as in the illustration—which would usually prove ineffectual.

57. Foot Twist, on the Floor.

Catch his foot and twist until he turns. Then

drop on his other leg and force the points down unless he admits the fall. Another form of punishment from this position is to drop your knee on his back, then bend his knee and twist. Look out for kicking from his free foot. Both this and No. 59 are used for making a man turn when he persists in lying face down.

58. An application of No. 57.

59. Head Hold and Twist.

Catch his chin and head, and twist. Punishment.

60. Lift from the Floor

Seldom used except in Græco-Roman wrestling. Lift him up and drop him on his shoulders as in No. 62.

61. Continuation of No. 60.

62. Fall from the Preceding

To Stop it, grasp his legs.

63. Double Front Elbows.

Try for a Both Legs Lock. To Stop it he will

probably grasp you about the waist. If he does so straighten up and throw him over your back, as in 64.

64. Continuation of No. 63.

65. Opposite Arm Hold, on the Floor.

Feint for a Half Nelson, grasp his opposite arm near the shoulder with both hands, roll him over and fall with him. To Stop it, Bridge and spin over on your face.

WHAT A WRESTLER NEEDS

A wrestler's apparel consists of Spalding full length tights. which can be obtained for $1.00 per pair in sanitary cotton, $2.50 in cut worsted, and $4.50 in best worsted. The Spalding No. WA wrestling full tights are made especially for the purpose after the suggestions and ideas of prominent wrestlers, including Gotch, Oleson and others. The best worsted is used, knit to shape, put together by hand and reinforced at knees with strong, silk finish worsted. They are made in colors black, navy blue and maroon, and cost $6.00 per pair. It is well to have the knees covered with protectors, which are to be sewn on the tights. These are inexpensive, ranging in price from 75 cents a pair for the best (No. B), which are covered with soft tanned horsehide and padded with hair felt, to 50 cents for tanned leather, nicely padded (No. 62), and 25 cents for durable cloth, padded with wool felt (No. 61).

No. B.

Nos. 61 and 62.

A jersey is desirable, which costs from $1.25 to $4.00, according to quality, and a pair of strong leather or canvas high cut gymnasium shoes. These latter cost from $1.00 to $1.75 for canvas and up to $5.00 for leather, the latter being of kangaroo with elkskin sole, extra light, and hand made. A very useful adjunct to a wrestler's outfit is the Spalding combined wrestling supporter and belt. It is made of mercerized silk elastic, strong and durable, and is the only really safe supporter for wrestling made. It costs $2.00 each. A bath robe is also essential, to prevent catching cold, and costs from $2.50 up.

Every wrestler should wear a supporter, to avoid injury. These can be bought from 20 cents up to $1.50, depending upon quality and construction. Bandages for the shoulder cap, knee cap, wrist, elbow or ankle can be obtained in silk or cotton. The elbow, knee and ankle bandages cost $1.50 each in cotton and $2.25 in silk; a wrist bandage, 75 cents in cotton and $1.00 in silk, and a shoulder cap, $4.50 in cotton and $6.00 in silk. A roll elastic bandage, 5 yards long and 3 inches wide, costs $1.00; the same length, but 2½ inches wide, 75 cents. Leather wrist supporters cost from 20 cents to 50 cents each.

Spalding's catalogue of athletic goods contains full descriptions, pictures and prices of all the above goods and everything for athletic wear and use, and will be mailed to any address free upon request. Address the Spalding store nearest to you for a copy, for list of which see inside front cover of this book.

Spalding Running Pants

Specify size and color when ordering

No. 1. White or Black Sateen, fly front, lace back. Pair, **$1.25** ★ *$12.00 Doz*
No. 2. White or Black Sateen, fly front, lace back. Pair, **$1.00** ★ *$10.00 Doz*.
No. 3. White or Black Silesia, fly front, lace back. Pair, **75c.** ★ *$7.80 Doz.*
No. 4. White, Black or Gray Silesia, fly front, lace back. Pair, **50c.** ★ *$5.00 Doz.*
No. 44. Same quality as No 4, but in juvenile sizes, not over 26 inch waist. Pair, **45c.**
Silk Ribbon Stripes down sides of any of these running pants. Pair, extra, **25c.** ★ *$2.40 Doz.*
Silk Ribbon Stripe around waist on any of these running pants. Pair, extra, **25c.** ★ *$2.40 Doz.*

Spalding Boys' Knee Pants

No. 2B. Boys' Leaders. Blue flannel Y.M.C.A. Knee Pants, stripe down side. Per pair, **$2.50**
No. 14B. Boys' Knee Pants, same quality as No. 4 Y.M.C.A. trousers, with stripe down side. Pair, **$1.00** ★ *$10.80 Doz.*

Spalding Worsted Trunks

No. 1. Best worsted, Black, Maroon, and Navy. Pair, **$2.00**
No. 2. Good quality worsted, Navy and Black. Special colors to order. Pr., **$1.00**

No. 1 Trunks

Spalding Velvet Trunks

No. 3. Fine Velvet. Black, Navy, Royal Blue, Maroon. Special colors to order. Pair, **$1.00** ★ *$10.00 Dz.*
No. 4. Sateen, Black, White. Pair, **50c.** ★ *$5.00 Doz.*

No. 3

Spalding Full Length Tights

No. 1A. Best worsted, full fashioned. Stock colors. Black, Navy Blue, Maroon. Sizes, 28 to 42 inch waist. Pair, **$4.00**
No. 605. Good quality worsted, stock colors and sizes. Pair, **$2.00** ★ *$21.60 Doz.*
No. 3A. Cotton, full quality. White, Black, Flesh. Pair, **$1.00** ★ *$10.00 Doz.*

[Wre]stling Full Tights

[carr]ied in stock. [S]pecial Orders only.
[Wo]rsted, knit to shape and [h]and. Reinforced at [lon]g silk finish wor[st]ed, Navy Blue, [Siz]es, waist, 28 [and o]ther colors [q]uoted on [$]6.00

Y.M.C.A. Trousers

Special Wrestling Mattresses

Cover heavy quality duck, closely tufted, 2 in. thick. Corduroy cover to lay over mat and allow 6-in. margin on all sides.
No. WX. Size 12x12 feet.
No. WXX. Size 15x15 feet.

Special Combined Wrestling Supporter and Belt

No WS. Mercerized silk elastic, strong and durable. The only safe supporter for wrestling. Each, **$2.00**

Spalding Y.M.C.A. Trousers
REGULATION STYLE

No. 2. Men's Leaders. Blue or Gray flannel, stripe down side. Per pair, **$3.50**
No. 3. Flannel, good quality." **3.00**
No. 4. Flannel, medium quality. Per pair, **$1.75** ★ *$18.00 Doz.*

Spalding Special Pads for Wrestling
To be Sewn on Wrestling Tights.

No. B. Soft tanned horse hide cover, hair felt padding. Per pair, **75c.**
No. 62. Covered with tan leather, padded. Pair, **50c.**
No. 61. Cloth covered, padded with wool felt. Per pair, **25c.**

No. B   Nos. 61 and 62

rices printed in italics will be quoted on orders of one-half dozen or more at one time. No reduction from regular retail prices on quantities of less than one-half dozen.

Athletic Shirts, Tights and Trunks

STOCK COLORS AND SIZES. OUR WORSTED GOODS are furnished in Gray, White, Navy Blue, Maroon, and Black only. Stock sizes: Shirts, 26 to 44 inch chest. Tights, 28 to 42 inch waist.
SANITARY COTTON GOODS. Colors: Bleached White, Navy, Black, Maroon, and Gray. Stock sizes: Shirts, 26 to 44 inch chest. Tights, 26 to 42 inch waist.

Spalding Sleeveless Shirts—Plain Colors
STOCK COLORS AND SIZES
No. 600. Good quality worsted. Each, $1.25 ★ $12.60 Doz.
No. 6E. Sanitary Cotton. . . " .50 ★ 4.75 "

Spalding Striped Sleeveless Shirts
No. 600S. Good quality worsted, with 6-inch stripe around chest, in following combinations of colors: Navy with White stripe; Black with Orange stripe; Maroon with White stripe; Red with Black stripe; Royal Blue with White Stripe; Black with Red stripe; Gray with Cardinal stripe.
Each, $1.50 ★ $15.00 Doz.
No. 6ES. Sanitary Cotton, solid color body, with 6-inch stripe around chest, in same combinations of colors as No. 600S.
Each, 75c. ★ $7.50 Doz.

No. 600S

Spalding Shirts with Sash
No. 600D. Good quality worsted, sleeveless, with woven sash of different color from body. Same colors as No. 600S. To order only; not carried in stock. Each, $2.00 ★ $21.00 Doz.
No. 6WD. Sanitary Cotton, sleeveless, with woven sash of different color from body. Same combinations of colors as No. 600S. To order only; not carried in stock.
Each, $1.25 ★ $12.00 Doz.
No. 6ED. Sanitary Cotton, sleeveless, solid color body with sash stitched on of different color. Same combinations of colors as No. 600S. . . . . . Each, 75c. ★ $7.50 Doz.

Spalding Quarter Sleeve Shirts
No. 601. Good quality worsted, stock colors and sizes. Each, $1.50 ★ $15.00 Doz.
No. 6F. Sanitary Cotton, stock colors and sizes. Each, 50c. ★ $4.75 Doz.

No. 601

Spalding Full Sleeve Shirts
No. 3D. Cotton, Flesh, White, Black. Ea., $1.00 ★ $10.00 Doz.

Spalding Knee Tights
STOCK COLORS AND SIZES
No. 604. Good quality worsted. Pair, $1.25 ★ $12.60 Doz.
No. 804. Worsted. " 1.00 ★ 10.80 "
No. 4B. Sanitary Cotton. . . " .50 ★ 4.75 "

Spalding Full Length Tights
No. 1A. Best worsted, full fashioned. Stock colors: Black, Navy Blue, and Maroon. Sizes, 28 to 42 inch waist. Pr., $4.00
No. 605. Good quality worsted, stock colors and sizes.
Pair, $2.00 ★ $21.60 Doz.
No. 3A. Cotton, full quality. White, Black, Flesh.
Pair, $1.00 ★ $10.00 Doz.

Spalding Worsted Trunks
No. 1. Best worsted, Black, Maroon, and Navy. Pair, $2.00
No. 2. Good quality worsted, Navy and Black. Special colors to order. . . . . Per pair, $1.00

Spalding Juvenile Shirts and Tights
ONLY SIZES SUPPLIED: Chest, 26 to 30 inches, inclusive; Waist, 24 to 26 inches, inclusive.
No. 65. Sleeveless Shirt, quality of No. 600. . Each, $1.00
No. 65S. Sleeveless Shirt, quality of No. 600S. . " 1.25
No. 66. Quarter Sleeve Shirt, quality of No. 601. " 1.25
No. 64. Knee Tights, quality of No. 604. . Pair, 1.15

The prices printed in italics opposite items marked with ★ will be quoted only on orders for one-half dozen or more. Quantity prices NOT allowed on items NOT marked with ★

Full Tights

SANDOW'S
ent Spring Grip Dumb Bell

tire system of Physical :ure is embraced within the :cises possible with these l dumb bells.

ls are made in two halves by steel springs, the effort in gripping compelling the ontinually devote his whole ach movement. This con- of will power on each olved is what is responsible at results obtained through xercising with them.

EUGEN SANDOW, PATENTEE

No. **6. MEN'S.** Nickel-plate seven steel springs. Pair, **$3.**
No. **5. MEN'S.** Black enamel five steel springs. Per pair, **$2.**
No. **4. LADIES'.** Nickel-plat five steel springs. Per pair, **$2.**
No. **2. BOYS'.** Nickel-plat four steel springs. Per pair, **$2.**

Sandow Patent Spring Du Bells are used by all the great athletes in their training.

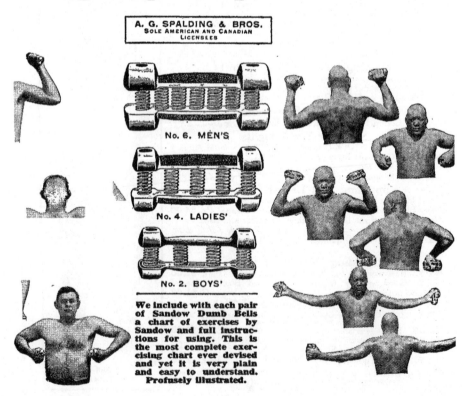

A. G. SPALDING & BROS.
SOLE AMERICAN AND CANADIAN LICENSEES

No. 6. MEN'S
No. 4. LADIES'
No. 2. BOYS'

We include with each pair of Sandow Dumb Bells a chart of exercises by Sandow and full instructions for using. This is the most complete exercising chart ever devised and yet it is very plain and easy to understand. **Profusely Illustrated.**

In effect July 5, 1912. Subject to change without notice. For Canadian prices see special Canadian Catalogue.

DING EXERCISING EQUIPMENT
For Recreation Rooms, Private Use and Small Athletic Clubs

BASE BALL TEAMS organized for the season only, disband usually until the following year unless something is done to keep the players together during the winter months. A moderate priced outfit of Spalding Exercising Apparatus installed in the club room provides the means for healthful recreation that insures a winning team on the base ball diamond next season.

Employers of office workers, banks and other mercantile establishments, find a Recreation Room fitted out with Spalding Exercising Equipment a most profitable investment. The room need not be very large, the size, of course, depending upon the number who are likely to use the room at the same time.

For the purpose of establishing a standard we would recommend a room 25 feet x 40 feet, with a minimum ceiling height of 16 feet. Recreative rooms can be maintained in smaller space, and excellent results can be obtained in rooms of 14 feet in height. Good air, with room for "group" games and medicine ball, boxing, etc., are desirable, however, and should be secured if possible.

No. G Home Outfit

Outfit No. G is arranged particularly for use in recreation room of a private hou... It provides a great variety of simple e...ercising apparatus at a very moder... cost. The equipment is suitable for u... by those of varying ages of both sex...

Consisting of:
1 No. 5 Chest Weight Machine.
1 No. 3 Head and Neck Attachm't.
1 No. 2 Foot and Leg Attachment.
1 No. 20H Bar Stall.
1 No. 205 Bar Stall Bench.
1 No. A Doorway Horizontal Bar.
1 No. 1 Home Gymnasium.
1 No. 600 Kerns' Row. Machine.
1 No. PR Striking Bag Disk.
1 No. 10 Striking Bag.
1 No. 1 Abdominal Masseur.
1 pair No. 6 Sandow Dumb Bells.
1 pair No. 2 Sandow Dumb Bells.
1 No. 02 Mattress.
1 No. 12 Medicine Ball.

Price is F.O.B. nearest A. G. Spalding & B... Store. List on inside front cover of catalog... Shipping weight of complete outfit, 450 l...

H Recreation Room Outfit

...o. H, referred to below, is suggested ...xclusively for recreation rooms, ...itable for use by those of vary... s, with sufficient equipment ...o supply as many as are likely to ...the room at the same time under circumstances, while additional ...ent may be added as required to ...of a larger number without dis... ...g the balance of the outfit.

onsisting of:
... Chest Weight Machine.
...ead and Neck Attachm't.
3 Swing Rings, leather cov...
Laflin Rowing Machine.
Moline Platform.
Striking Bag.
...all Horizont. and Vault. Bar.
Mattress.
...o. 6 Sandow Dumb Bells.
...o. 5 Sandow Dumb Bells.
15 Boxing Gloves.
118 Boxing Gloves.
Medicine Ball.
Medicine Ball.

...O.B. nearest A. G. Spalding & Bros.
...ist on inside front cover of catalogue.
...weight of complete outfit, 570 lbs.

Showing suggested arrangement of apparatus included in Outfit H

No. K Athletic Club Outfit

onsisting of
... Chest Weight Machines.
... Head and Neck Attachment.
... Foot and Leg Attachment.
... H Bar Stalls.
...0 Kerns' Rowing Machine.
...o 3 Swinging Rings, leather covered.
...o 3 Swinging Rings, leather covered.
...ing rings, 40 ft. length of room required, 15 to 16 ft. height)
... Moline Striking Bag Platform
... Striking Bag.
... Wall Horizontal and Vaulting Bar.
1 Parallel Bar.
... Mattresses.
...o. 6 Sandow Dumb Bells
...o. 5 Sandow Dumb Bells.
...o. 2 Sandow Dumb Bells.
. 218 Boxing Gloves.
. 118 Boxing Gloves.
... Medicine Ball.
... Medicine Ball.
...-lb. Iron Dumb Bells.
5-lb. Iron Dumb Bell.
0-lb. Iron Dumb Bell.

...B. nearest A. G. Spalding & Bros. Store. List on inside front ...is catalogue. Shipping weight of complete outfit, 1250 lbs.

No. J Athletic Club Outfit

Consisting of:
1 No. 5 Chest Weight Machine.
1 No. 3 Head and Neck Attachment.
1 No. 2 Foot and Leg Attachment.
1 No. 20H Bar Stall.
1 No. 600 Kerns' Rowing Machine.
1 air No. 3 Swinging Rings, leather covered.
1 p o. 74 Wall Horizontal and Vaulting Bar
2 No. 03 Mattresses.
1 No. 1 Moline Striking Bag Platform.
1 No. G Striking Bag.
1 set No. 15 Boxing Gloves.
1 set No. 118 Boxing Gloves.
2 pairs No. 6 Sandow Dumb Bells.
1 pair No. 5 Sandow Dumb Bells.
1 pair No. 2 Sandow Dumb Bells.
1 No. 12 Medicine Ball.
1 No. 11 Medicine Ball.

Price F.O.B. nearest A. G. Spalding & Bros. Store. List on inside fro... cover of this catalogue. Shipping weight of complete outfit, 725 lb...
NOTE—Where space and funds permit we recommend as a desirab... addition to either of the above Outfits, one of our special Wrestli... Mats, listed on page 41 of this catalogue:

No. WX. Size 12 x 12 feet.
No. WXX. Size 15 x 15 feet.
Also Vaulting Horse No. 1 (Shown on page 102).

ding "Championship" Boxing Gloves

alding Boxing Gloves have been used and endorsed by all
ampions of the World since the days of John L. Sullivan

"Championship" Boxing Gloves are endorsed by all champions and have
ely used for years in championship contests and in training. The material
ship are of the highest quality, the fit is perfect, and by their peculiar con-
olutely prevent any chance of injury to the hands or wrists. Each set is
ected before packing and guaranteed in every particular. Made in three
sizes in sets of four gloves.
ll Spalding Boxing Gloves are Hair Filled. No cotton or carpet flock used.

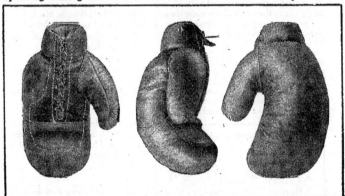 

e Spalding 5-oz. "Championship" Boxing Glove. Per set of 4 gloves, **$6.00**
e Spalding 6-oz. "Championship" Boxing Glove. Per set of 4 gloves, **6.00**
e Spalding 8-oz. "Championship" Boxing Glove. Per set of 4 gloves, **7.00**

Spalding "Special" Boxing Shoes

Hand Made. Light Weight.

No. 15

These shoes are made with elkskin soles, which do not wear smooth. This style leather is the only kind that is suitable for a first-class boxing shoe sole. The uppers are of real kangaroo leather, pliable and very easy fitting. Being made by hand and of best quality materials throughout, these shoes are very durable, yet at the same time they are the lightest in weight of any.

No. 15. Spalding "Special" Boxing Shoes. Pair, **$5.00**

alding Boxing Gloves

All Spalding Boxing Gloves are hair filled. No cotton or carpet flock used

The Spalding 6-ounce "Battling" Glove
None Better at Any Price

No. 106. Made of special quality light tan colored glove leather, very soft and smooth. Plain laced wrist-band, patent palm lacing and patent palm grip. An ideal glove for limited round contests. A popular glove with some of the greatest fighters in the ring during the past twenty years.
Per set of four gloves, $7.00

Spalding Pupil's Boxing Glove

No. 110. Made after the suggestion of one of the most prominent athletic officials in this country. A boxing glove that is really an aid to the pupil learning to box. This glove is additionally padded on the forearm and over the wrist, to prevent that soreness which is one of the most discouraging features following a brisk lesson in the art of "blocking." The glove part is well padded with curled hair, the leather being best quality soft tanned.
Per set of four gloves, $6.50

No. 110

Spalding Instructors' Glove, 10-ounce

No 100. Made of best grade brown leather, extra heavily padded over the knuckles and with special large padded thumb to prevent injury to either instructor or pupil. Laces extra far to provide ample ventilation and has patent palm grip. . . . . Per set of four gloves, $6.00

Spalding "Navy Special" Championship Glove
Used by the Champions of the Navy

Showing Padding on Wrist and Forearm of No. 110

BOXING IN THE NAVY
Copyright, 1905, by G. W. Fawcett, Washington, D. C.

No. 18N. Made of a special "sea-green" leather, of particularly durable quality. This glove we got up specially to answer the requirements of the United States Navy. Furnished in 8-ounce only, similar in style to No. 118, and with padded wrist and laced wrist band. Set of four gloves, $5.50

Spalding "Club Special" No. 218

No. 218. Full size, 8-ounce. Same model as our "Championship" Glove No. 118. Good quality glove leather and careful workmanship. Superior to any of the gloves put out by other manufacturers in imitation of our Championship styles. . . . . Per set of four gloves, $5.00

No. 218

NG BOXING GL

STYLES FOR SPORTING AND ATHLETIC CLUBS

No. 11

Illustrating Patent Elastic Hand Protector, same as we are including in our Nos. 9E and 14E Gloves. Prevents injury to hands.

All Spalding Boxing Gloves are Hair Filled. No Cotton or Carpet Flock Used.

No. 11. Corbett pattern, large 7-oz. glove, best quality brown leather, padded with best curled hair, patent palm lacing, padded wristband, patent palm grip. Substantially made throughout for hard usage. . . Set of four gloves, **$5.00**

No. 9. Regulation 5-oz. glove, otherwise same as No. 11 Glove. This glove is a better article than what other manufacturers supply for limited round contests. . . Set of four gloves, **$5.00**

o. **9E.** Patented elastic hand protector in gloves. Otherwise as No. 9. Set of four gloves, $

o. **14.** Regulation 5-oz. glove, Brown glove leather, improved model; special padded thumb, nd heel, patent palm lacing, palm grip. Used by some of the best organizations for their ontests. . . . . Set of four gloves, $

o. **14E.** Patented elastic hand protector in gloves. Otherwise as No. 14.

Spalding Boxing Gloves
Styles for Friendly Bouts and Private Use

o. **15.** Corbett pattern, 8-oz., olive tanned ather, well padded with hair, padded wrist- and, patent palm lacing, patent palm grip. Set of four gloves, **$4.00**

o. **17.** Corbett pattern, 7-oz., dark wine color leather, hair padded, patent palm lacing, patent palm rip, padded wristband. Set of four gloves, **$4.00**

o. **19.** Corbett pattern, 7-oz., dark wine color ather, padded with hair, patent palm grip and atent palm lacing. . Set of four gloves, **$3.50**

Spalding Boxing Glove
Styles for Practice and Amateur Use

No. 21. Corbett pattern, 8-oz., dark wine leather. Full size, well padded with hair, patent palm lacing. . . Set of four gloves, $

No. 23. Corbett pattern, brown tanned lea Hair padded and patent palm lacing. Set of four gloves, $

No. 24. Regular pattern, tan leather, hair ded, and has laced wristband. Set of four gloves, $

ding Youths' Boxing Gloves
All Styles Padded with Hair. No Cotton or Carpet Flock Used

No. 45

Spalding Youths' Boxing Gloves are made in exactly the same manner and of s material to the full size gloves of our manufacture and are warranted to give satisfa

No. 45. Youths' Championship Glove, Corbett pattern, best quality b glove leather, extra well finished, double stitched, patent palm lacing, p palm grip. . . . . Set of four gloves, $

No. 40. Youths' size, Corbett pattern, soft craven tan leather, well pad patent palm lacing. . . . . Set of four gloves, $

No. 25. Youths' size, regular pattern, soft tanned leather, patent lacing. . . . . Set of four gloves, $

EACH SET OF SPALDING BOXING GLOVES CONSISTS OF FOUR GL MATED IN TWO PAIRS

Prices in effect July 5, 1912. Subject to change without notice. For Canadian prices see special Canadian Catalogu

The Spalding Striking

Our single end bags are made with rope attachment carefully centered, making them the most cer Laces on side at top, so that the bladder may be inflated without interfering with rope. Each b inspected and then packed complete in box with bladder, lace and rope.

The bladders used in all our striking bags are made of pure Para rubber (not compounded) and are fully guaranteed.

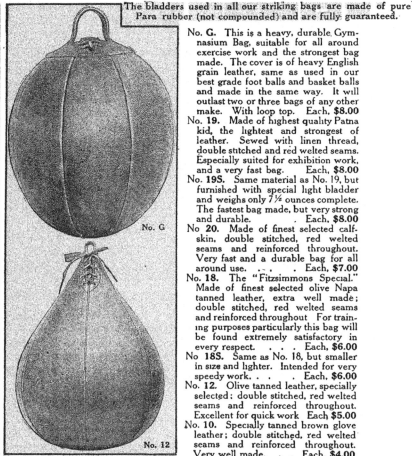

No. G
No. 12

No. G. This is a heavy, durable Gymnasium Bag, suitable for all around exercise work and the strongest bag made. The cover is of heavy English grain leather, same as used in our best grade foot balls and basket balls and made in the same way. It will outlast two or three bags of any other make. With loop top. Each, $8.00

No. 19. Made of highest quality Patna kid, the lightest and strongest of leather. Sewed with linen thread, double stitched and red welted seams. Especially suited for exhibition work, and a very fast bag. Each, $8.00

No. 19S. Same material as No. 19, but furnished with special light bladder and weighs only 7½ ounces complete. The fastest bag made, but very strong and durable. Each, $8.00

No 20. Made of finest selected calfskin, double stitched, red welted seams and reinforced throughout. Very fast and a durable bag for all around use. Each, $7.00

No. 18. The "Fitzsimmons Special." Made of finest selected olive Napa tanned leather, extra well made; double stitched, red welted seams and reinforced throughout For training purposes particularly this bag will be found extremely satisfactory in every respect. Each, $6.00

No 18S. Same as No. 18, but smaller in size and lighter. Intended for very speedy work. Each, $6.00

No. 12. Olive tanned leather, specially selected; double stitched, red welted seams and reinforced throughout. Excellent for quick work Each $5.00

No. 10. Specially tanned brown glove leather; double stitched, red welted seams and reinforced throughout. Very well made. Each, $4.00

No. 17. Fine craven tanned leather, well finished; double stitched, red welted seams, reinforced throughout. $3.50

No. 16. Extra fine grain leather, full size and lined throughout; welted seams. Each, $3.00

No. 15. Made of oli throughout; red we

No. 14. Good quali out.

SPALDING STRIKING BAG SW

No. 4

No. 4. A special swivel, made according to suggestions of experienced bag punchers, with features that overcome disadvantages of ordinary style. Rope can be changed instantly without interfering with any other part of swivel, Each, $1.50

No. 9. With removable socket for quickly suspending or removing bag without readjusting. Each, 50c.

No. 6. Japanned iron stem for use with platform or disk. " 35c.

No. 12. Ball and Socket action. Fastens permanently to disk; nickel-plated.

SPALDING DOUBLE END BAG

All double end striking bags are supplied complete with guaranteed pure gum bladder, rubber cord floor, lace for bag and rope for ceiling attachment.

No. 7. Made of finest selected olive Napa tanned leather, workmanship of same quality as in our "Fitzsimmons" Special Bag No. 18. Double stitched, red welted seams An extremely durable and lively bag. . . Each, **$6.00**
No. 6. Fine olive tanned leather cover, double stitched, red welted seams. Extra well made throughout. . . . . . Each, **$5.50**
No. 5. Regulation size, specially tanned brown glove leather cover, red welted seams, double stitched and substantially made throughout. . . . Each, **$5.00**
No. 4½. Regulation size, fine craven tanned leather and red welted seams. Well finished throughout. Each, **$4.00**
No. 4. Regulation size, fine grain leather ver, well made throughout, double stitched Ea., **$3.50**
.3 Regulation size, substantial brown leather cover, nforced and double stitched seams. . Each, **$3.00**
.2½. Regulation size, good quality dark olive tanned ther, lined throughout, red welted seams. Ea., **$2.00**
. 2. Medium size, good colored sheepskin, lined oughout. . . . . Each, **$1.50**

lding Bladders
Bladders used in all our Striking Bags are made of pure Para rubber (not compou are fully guaranteed. Note special explanation of guarantee on tag attached to ea

No. B. For Nos. 2, 2½, 3, 14 and 15 Ea., **75c.**
No. 5. For Nos. 4, 4½, 5, 6. 10, 12, 16 and 17 . . . Each, **90c.**
No. 7 For Nos. 7, 18, 18S, 19, 19S and 20. Each, **$1.00**
No. G. For No. G Bag. . . . " **2.00**

No. OS. With top stem, heavy b special quality. . . . . . Each,
No. D. Elastic floor attachment for all end bags, best quality cord. . Eac
No. E. Elastic cord for double end b Eac

Spalding Brass Inflaters

Club size, cylinder 10½ inches. . . . Each, **50c.**
Pocket size, cylinder 5½ inches. . . " **25c.**

Spalding Striking Bag Mitts
Will protect the hands and recommen for use with all Striking Bags

No. 1. Made of olive Napa leather and extra well padded; ventilate and special elastic wrist in glove. . . . . . . Pair,
No. 2. Made of soft tanned leather, properly shaped and padded, s tially put together . . . . Pair,
No. 3. Made of soft tanned leather, padded and wel also made in ladies' size. . . . . . . P
No. 4. Knuckle Mitt, well padded. . . . .
No. 5. Knuckle Mitt, well padded. . . . . .

SPALDING
NT SOLID STRIKING BAG DISKS

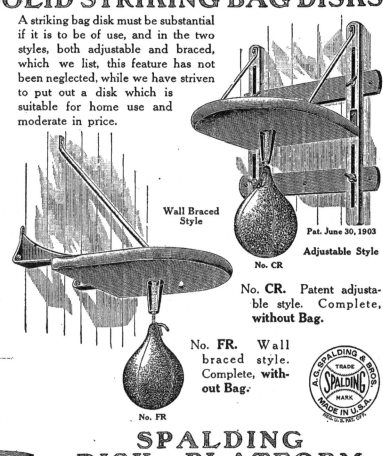

A striking bag disk must be substantial if it is to be of use, and in the two styles, both adjustable and braced, which we list, this feature has not been neglected, while we have striven to put out a disk which is suitable for home use and moderate in price.

Wall Braced Style

Pat. June 30, 1903

Adjustable Style

No. CR

No. **CR.** Patent adjustable style. Complete, **without Bag.**

No. **FR.** Wall braced style. Complete, **without Bag.**

No. FR

SPALDING
DISK PLATFORM

Can be put up in a very small space and taken down quickly when not in use by simply detaching the pipe fixture from the wall plate. The metal disk against which the bag strikes constitutes one of the best features ever incorporated in an arrangement of this character, rendering it almost noiseless and very quick in action. This disk also combines an adjustable feature that is simple to operate and makes it possible for various members of the family to use the same disk.

No. **PR.** Spalding Adjustable Disk Platform. Complete **with bag.**

ACCEPT NO SUBSTITUTE THE SPALDING TRADE-MARK **GUARANTEES QUALITY**

Spalding "Official National League" Ball
(REG. U.S. PAT. OFF.)

Patent Cork Center
(PATENTED AUGUST 31, 1909)

Adopted by the National League in 1878, is the only ball used in Championship games since that time and has now been adopted for twenty years more, making a total adoption of fifty-four years.

In adopting the Spalding "Official National League" Ball for twenty years more the Secretary of the National League, Mr. John A. Heydler, gave the following as the reason for this action:

"The Spalding Ball was adopted by the National League for twenty years, because we recognized it as the best ball made. We have used it satisfactorily for thirty-four years. The new Cork Center Ball introduced for the first time last year and used in the World's Series, we believe to be the only ball for the future, and it is absolutely the best that has been used by the National League in its history."

This ball has the Spalding "Patent" Cork Center, the same as used since August 1, 1910, without change in size of cork or construction.

No. 1 { Each, - - $1.25
Per Dozen, $15.00

Each ball wrapped in tinfoil, packed in a separate box, and sealed in accordance with the latest League regulations. Warranted to last a full game when used under ordinary conditions.

The Spalding "Official National League" Ball has been the Official Ball of the Game since 1878

Spalding Complete Catalogue of Athletic Goods Mailed Free.

PROMPT ATTENTION GIVEN TO ANY COMMUNICATIONS ADDRESSED TO US   **A. G. SPALDING & BROS.** STORES IN ALL LARGE CITIES   **COMPLETE LIST OF STORES ON INSIDE FRONT COVER OF THIS BOOK**

Prices in effect January 5, 1912. Subject to change without notice. For Canadian prices see special Canadian Catalogue.

ollowing selection of items from Spalding's latest Catalogue will giv
a of the great variety of **ATHLETIC GOODS** manufactured b
SPALDING & BROS.   SEND FOR A FREE COP

See list of Spalding Stores on inside front cover of this book.

	PAGE		PAGE		PAGE		PAGE		PAG
Skate	62	Emblems	43, 44	Jackets—		Platforms, Striking Bag	92, 93	Skates—	
er	11	Embroidery	43	Fencing	108	Poles—		Ice	51.
ry	110, 111	Exercisers—		Foot Ball	8	Ski	50	Roller	
		Elastic	106	Javelins	74	Vaulting	74	Skate Bag	
st Weight	98, 99	Home	106	Jerseys	21-23	Polo Roller, Goods	66	Skate Keys	62.
		Equestrian Polo	69			Protectors—		Skate Straps	
				Knee Protectors	39, 68	Abdomen	12, 66	Skate Sundries	
				Knickerbockers, Foot Ball	19	Eyeglass	65	Skis	
		Felt Letters	44			Finger, Field Hockey	72	Snow Shoes	
	82	Fencing Sticks	107			Indoor Base Ball	68	Sprint Lanes	
	90, 91	Finger Protection, Hockey	72			Knee	68	Squash Goods	
	62	Flags—				Thumb, Basket Ball	37	Standards—	
		College	45	Lace, Foot Ball	7	Protection, Running Shoes	78	Vaulting	
	109	Marking, Golf	84	Lacrosse Goods	69	Pucks, Hockey, Ice	64	Volley Ball	
	36, 37	Foils, Fencing	107	Fencing Goods	107, 108	Push Ball	71	Straps—	
	72	Foot Balls—		Field Hockey Goods	72	Pushers, Chamois	78	For Three-Legged Race	
y	3-6	Association	17, 18	Gymnasium Shoes	33, 34			Skate	
e	16	College	3-6	Gymnasium Suits	29-32			Sticks, Roller Polo	
	17, 18	Rugby	16	Skates, Ice	51-59			Stockings	
	79	Skates Roller	67					Foot Ball	
	70	Foot Ball Clothing	8	Skating Shoes	60, 61	Quoits	71	Stop Boards	
	72	Foot Ball Goal Nets	18	Snow Shoes	49			Striking Bags	90,
	68	Foot Ball Timer	7	Lanes for Sprints	75			Suits—	
	69			Leg Guards—				Base Ball, Indoor	
	70			Foot Ball	10, 19			Gymnasium, Ladies'	29-
	68			Ice Hockey	65	Racks, Golf Ball	84	Soccer	
	66	Gloves—		Polo, Roller	66	Racquet, Squash	96	Swimming	
	46	Boxing	87, 89	Letters—		Rapiers, Fencing	107	Water Polo	11, 1
	71	Fencing	108	Embroidered	43	Referee's Whistle	37, 75	Supporters	
	86	Golf	83	Felt	43, 44	Rings—		Ankle	
	71	Handball	70	Liniment, "Mike Murphy"	13	Exercising	104	Wrist	
Golf	83	Hockey Field	72			Swinging	104	Suspensories	
stic	13	Hockey Ice	64			Rowing Machines	100	Sweaters	24-
	95	Lacrosse	69	Masks—				Swivels, Striking Bags	
	105	Goals—		Fencing	108			Swords, Fencing	10
	101, 102	Basket Ball	38	Nose	10			Swords, Duelling	10
	102	Foot Ball	18	Masseur, Abdominal	105				
	68	Hockey Field	72	Mattresses, Gymnasium	104				
	68	Hockey Ice	64	Mattresses, Wrestling	41	Sacks, for Sack Racing	75	Tackling Machine	
		Lacrosse	69	Megaphones	7	Sandals, Snow Shoe	49	Take-Off Board	7
	8	Goal Cage Roller Polo	66	Mitts—		Sandow & Dumb Bells	94	Tape, Measuring, Steel	7
Worsted	11	Golf Clubs	80, 81	Handball	70	Scabbards, Skate	62	Tees, Golf	8
	41	Golf Sundries	83, 84	Striking Bag	91	Score Books—		Posts, Tennis, Indoor	
		Colfette	84	Moccasins	49	Basket Ball	37	Tights—	
	37	Grips—		Monograms	43, 44	Shin Guards—		Full	
	7, 16, 18	Athletic	78	Mouthpiece, Foot Ball	10	Association	19	Full, Wrestling	
	91	Golf	83	Mufflers, Knitted	27	College	10	Hockey	
g	107	Gymnasium, Home	97			Field Hockey	72	Knee	
		Gymnasium Board, Home	105			Ice Hockey	65	Toboggans	
		Gymnasium, Home Outfits	103	Needle, Lacing	7	Polo, Roller	66	Toboggan Cushions	
				Nets—		Shirts—		Toe Boards	
	84			Basket Ball	38	Athletic	40	Toques	
		Hammers, Athletic	73	Golf Driving	84	Rubber Reducing	46	Trapeze, Adjustable	
	69	Hangers for Dumb Bells	96	Volley Ball	71	Shoes—		Trapeze, Single	
	42	Hangers for Indian Clubs	96	Numbers, Competitor's	74	Acrobatic	34	Trousers—	
	19, 48	Hats, University	42			Basket Ball	34, 35	Y.M.C.A.	4
	42	Head Harness	10, 16			Clog	35	Foot Ball	
	46	Health Pull	106			Fencing	108	Trunks—	
	98, 99	Hob Nails	85	Pads—		Foot Ball Association	18	Velvet	4
oot	75	Hockey Pucks	64	Chamois, Fencing	108	Foot Ball College	14-15	Worsted	4
tied	84	Hockey Sticks, Ice	63, 64	Foot Ball	9	Foot Ball, Rugby	16		
g	27	Hockey Sticks, Field	72	Wrestling	41	Foot Ball Soccer	18		
ulting	78	Holder, Basket Ball, Canvas	37	Paint, Golf	83	Shoes—			
	74	Hole Cutter, Golf	84	Pants—		Golf	85	Uniforms—	
		Hole Rim, Golf	84	Basket Ball	39	Gymnasium	33, 34	Base Ball, Indoor	
		Horse, Vaulting	102	Boys Knee	39	Jumping	76-78		
		Hurdles, Safety	75	Foot Ball, College	8	Running	76-78		
		Hurley Sticks	72	Foot Ball, Rugby	16	Skating	60, 61		
ic	74			Hockey, Ice	65	Snow	49		
				Running	41	Squash	86	Wands, Calisthenic	
If	84	Indian Clubs	96	Pennants, College	45	Street	47	Watches, Stop	
Shoe	83, 85	Inflaters—		Pistol, Starter's	75	Walking	76	Weights, 56-lb.	
Bag	92	Foot Ball	7	Plastrons, Fencing	108	Shot—		Whistles	37,
	94, 95	Striking Bag	91	Plates—		Athletic	73	Wrestling Equipment	
				Teeing, Golf	83	Indoor	73	Wrist Machines	1
						Massage	105		

DEC 13 1912

Standard Policy

A Standard Quality must be inseparably linked to a Standard Policy.

Without a definite and Standard Mercantile Policy, it is impossible for a Manufacturer to long maintain a Standard Quality.

To market his goods through a jobber, a manufacturer must provide a profit for the jobber as well as for the retail dealer. To meet these conditions of Dual Profits, the manufacturer is obliged to set a proportionately high list price on his goods to the consumer.

To enable the glib salesman, when booking his orders, to figure out attractive profits to both the jobber and retailer, these high list prices are absolutely essential; but their real purpose will have been served when the manufacturer has secured his order from the jobber, and the jobber has secured his order from the retailer.

However, these deceptive high list prices are not fair to the consumer, who does not, and, in reality, is not ever expected to pay these fancy list prices.

When the season opens for the sale of such goods, with their misleading but alluring high list prices, the retailer begins to realize his responsibilities, and grapples with the situation as best he can, by offering "special discounts," which vary with local trade conditions.

Under this system of merchandising, the profits to both the manufacturer and the jobber are assured; but as there is no stability maintained in the prices to the consumer, the keen competition amongst the local dealers invariably leads to a demoralized cutting of prices by which the profits of the retailer are practically eliminated.

This demoralization always reacts on the manufacturer. The jobber insists on lower, and still lower, prices. The manufacturer, in his turn, meets this demand for the lowering of prices by the only way open to him, viz.: the cheapening and degrading of the quality of his product.

The foregoing conditions became so intolerable that, 13 years ago, in 1899, A. G. Spalding & Bros. determined to rectify this demoralization in the Athletic Goods Trade, and inaugurated what has since become known as "The Spalding Policy."

The "Spalding Policy" eliminates the jobber entirely, so far as Spalding Goods are concerned, and the retail dealer secures the supply of Spalding Athletic Goods direct from the manufacturer by which the retail dealer is assured a fair, legitimate and certain profit on all Spalding Athletic Goods, and the consumer is assured a Standard Quality and is protected from imposition.

The "Spalding Policy" is decidedly for the interest and protection of the users of Athletic Goods, and acts in two ways:

First.—The user is assured of genuine Official Standard Athletic Goods and the same prices to everybody.

Second.—As manufacturers, we can proceed with confidence in purchasing at the proper time, the very best raw materials required in the manufacture of our various goods, well ahead of their respective seasons, and this enables us to provide the necesssary quantity and absolutely maintain the Spalding Standard of Quality.

All retail dealers handling Spalding Athletic Goods are requested to supply consumers at our regular printed catalogue prices—neither more nor less—the same prices that similar goods are sold for in our New York, Chicago and other stores.

All Spalding dealers, as well as users of Spalding Athletic Goods, are treated exactly alike, and no special rebates or discriminations are allowed to anyone.

This briefly, is the "Spalding Policy," which has already been in successful operation for the past 13 years, and will be indefinitely continued.

In other words, "The Spalding Policy" is a "square deal" for everybody.

A. G. SPALDING & BROS.

By *A. G. Spalding*,

PRESIDENT.

Standard Quality

An article that is universally given the appellation "Standard" is thereby conceded to be the criterion, to which are compared all other things of a similar nature. For instance, the Gold Dollar of the United States is the Standard unit of currency, because it must legally contain a specific proportion of pure gold, and the fact of its being Genuine is **guaranteed** by the Government Stamp thereon. As a protection to the users of this currency against counterfeiting and other tricks, considerable money is expended in maintaining a Secret Service Bureau of Experts. Under the law, citizen manufacturers must depend to a great extent upon Trade-Marks and similar devices to protect themselves against counterfeit products—without the aid of "Government Detectives" or "Public Opinion" to assist them.

Consequently the "Consumer's Protection" against misrepresentation and "inferior quality" rests entirely upon the integrity and responsibility of the "Manufacturer."

A. G. Spalding & Bros. have, by their rigorous attention to "Quality," for thirty-five years, caused their Trade-Mark to become known throughout the world as a Guarantee of Quality as dependable in their field as the U. S. Currency is in its field.

The necessity of upholding the Guarantee of the Spalding Trade-Mark and maintaining the Standard Quality of their Athletic Goods, is, therefore, as obvious as is the necessity of the Government in maintaining a Standard Currency.

Thus each consumer is not only insuring himself but also protecting other consumers when he assists a Reliable Manufacturer in upholding his Trade-Mark and all that it stands for. Therefore, we urge all users of our Athletic Goods to assist us in maintaining the Spalding Standard of Excellence, by insisting that our Trade-Mark be plainly stamped on all athletic goods which they buy, because without this precaution our best efforts towards maintaining Standard Quality and preventing fraudulent substitution will be ineffectual.

Manufacturers of Standard Articles invariably suffer the reputation of being high-priced, and this sentiment is fostered and emphasized by makers of "inferior goods," with whom low prices are the main consideration.

A manufacturer of recognized Standard Goods, with a reputation to uphold and a guarantee to protect, must necessarily have higher prices than a manufacturer of cheap goods, whose idea of and basis of a claim for Standard Quality depends principally upon the eloquence of the salesman.

We know from experience that there is no quicksand more unstable than poverty in quality—and we avoid this quicksand by Standard Quality.

A. G. Spalding & Bros.

CPSIA information can be obtained
at www.ICGtesting.com
Printed in the USA
BVOW08s0957161117
500586BV00018B/1048/P